LAMENTATIONS OF OUR HEART

A MELANCHOLY AND AMOROUS REVERIE

MAIRA KHAN

BookLeaf Publishing
India | USA | UK

Made with ❤ on the BookLeaf Publishing Platform
www.bookleafpub.in
www.bookleafpub.com

Dedication

For those who live in between the lines,

To the hearts that break and heal,

For the dreamers and the restless souls,

To the ones who listen with their hearts,

May these words offer you a place to rest,

And may these poems echo the silent truths within you.

THIS POEM IS DEDICATED TO THOSE SIX IDIOTS WHO MADE MY SCHOOL LIFE UNFORGETTABLE

THE TIMELESS BOND

In luminous corridors we once wandered,
Through substantial tomes, we crafted our sanctuary.
Laughter reverberated, hearts entwined,
Visions were sculpted, unrestrained and pure.

Now, the world has drawn us apart,
On distant shores, we each reside.
Amidst vibrant cities, sprawling meadows,
Pursuing aspirations yet uncharted.

Though time and distance may stretch us thin,
We carry each other, akin to guiding constellations.
In every triumph, in each setback,
I hear your voice; I feel your presence.

The bonds of friendship endure,
Unyielding in joy, steadfast through sorrow.
For though our journeys diverge with elegance,
In cherished memories, we remain united.

So here's to you, in uncharted fields,
With every step, you linger in my thoughts.
And when the path seems arduous and long,
Recall the echoes of our shared refrain.

Acknowledgement

I want to express my heartfelt gratitude to those who have supported me on this journey. I want to extend my deepest appreciation to my brother, Mohammad Rahat Khan. Your constant support, humor, and love have been a guiding light through the ups and downs of this process. Thank you for always being there, cheering me on, and reminding me of the joy of creating.

A special thank you to my dear friend, Saima Khalid, whose unwavering encouragement and insightful feedback have been invaluable in shaping these poems. Your belief in my work has inspired me more than words can convey.

And! Especially to the one with a quiet yet powerful presence in my life. Your silent strength, endless support, and belief in me have carried me through the most challenging moments. This book holds the imprints of your influence, and for that, I am eternally grateful.

This book is a reflection of our shared moments and the bonds we cherish. I am forever grateful to all of you.

Preface

In the intricate tapestry of human expression, poetry often emerges as the thread that binds our most fleeting thoughts to the permanence of ink and page. This collection, *Lamentations Of Our Heart*: a melancholy and amorous reverie, represents a series of verses and a mosaic of experiences, emotions, and reflections. It is a personal journey rendered in language, where each poem serves as a milestone and a map—charting the terrain of the heart and mind with a blend of precision and vulnerability.

This volume is more than a compilation; it is a passage through a labyrinth of emotions and insights, where each poem opens a doorway into a distinct facet of the human experience. These verses act as a compass and guide, navigating a landscape as diverse and complex as our inner lives.

The art of writing poetry is an intimate engagement with language, where every choice of word and rhythm is deliberate, aimed at capturing the essence of fleeting moments and timeless truths. I hope these poems offer a glimpse into my inner world and resonate with your own experiences and reflections.

As you turn these pages, may you find both solace and challenge—a space where you can confront your truths and uncover new dimensions of thought. I earnestly wish that this collection serves as both a mirror and beacon, guiding you through the depths of emotion and the heights of inspiration.

This preface introduces a work that is as much an exploration of language as an examination of the human psyche. I trust that these poems will offer a rich tapestry of imagery and insight, fostering both introspection and a deeper appreciation of the art form.

I invite you to immerse yourself in the world of these poems, to engage with the interplay of rhythm and thought, and to discover the resonances that lie within the folds of each verse.

1. THE SILENT OBSERVER

As I sit back and write another epitome of self-destruction,

The echoes of my laughter linger in the calmest of nights,

All my shattered dreams paint an abstract yet beautiful canvas,

Lies whispered my silent scream, dancing with the shadows of fallacy.

Lost in the maze of memories, my heart searches for a way back,

Amidst the black sky, the fragments of my shattered self make a constellation,

In the unity of chaos, my cries are no less than a haunting melody,

Yet, I remain the silent observer of our unraveling universe.

The whiskey-soaked regrets echo in my boudoir of confinement,

Sharp blades never inflict wounds as deep as the other person's words,

And so, I fade like the dying embers of a once-blazing fire,

As I sit back and write another epitome of self-destruction.

People consider me mad, lost, wandering, and I
don't know whatnot,

But why do they consider me so? Am I composed
of all such qualities?

Underneath my endless questions lie all the
answers in catastrophic chaos,

Yet, I remain the silent observer of our unraveling
universe.

2. OBSESSION

Obsession, a visionary of change, mold me into a query,

A puzzle with no solutions reveals the core of my being,

In the wreckage of hope, my sounds of happiness have been muted,

Remnants of previously shared laughter haunt my loneliness.

Amidst the debris of my feelings, I seek the reflection that shows who I've become,

A fragmented reflection stares back, marked by the choices made,

Obsession, the muse of my undoing, traces lines upon my heart,

Each line is a memory, a piece of what was and what could have been.

Obsession, the sculptor, shapes my pain into strength,

It carves a new path from the ruins of my disappointment,

With every beat of my heart, I reclaim pieces of myself,

Gaining strength from the echoes of a once cherished past.

Within this chaos, a flicker of hope defies the dark,

A spark that insists on the possibility of rebirth,

Through the ashes of despair, a Phoenix rises, wings aflame,

Transforming the echoes of laughter into a symphony of resilience.

And the grip of obsession was lost.

3. YEARNS OF MY HEART

I was shattered,

I felt on the ground as if I was the shards of glass that had just broken into pieces,

The tears dripped down just as the blood on those shards would,

But it all had to be imperceptible.

I felt as if I was in Commonwealth Bay,

Surrendering myself to the winds blowing from the east to the west,

I was as numb as someone about to be operated,

Waiting for the winds to carry me away and throw me somewhere to let me feel the pain.

The worst part was that I couldn't share it,

With a heart as heavy as lead,

I'd to bear the pain and let myself fall to pieces,

I'd like to be quiet and calm and survive until Azrael calls upon me and takes me to a better place.

4. A DREAM FULFILLED

His eyes are my favorite color,

They were orbs of brown with black specks,

His smile was always as free as a rose in summer air,

He was astounding and everything I wished love would be.

But he was sad.

He was a song as sad as the wild waves.

His mind was a conundrum.

He was a masterpiece of broken, blemished glass waiting to be fixed.

And so I tried, I took him to the beach with the waves that wrapped around him and hugged him.

I left him millions of positive reminiscences everywhere we went.

He told me not to even make an effort, and I made sure to remind him that having the blues is not the end of the world until he believed it.

And in the end, we pulled through, he was by my side, and I wouldn't have it any other way.

Happily ever after, I suppose.

5. WHISPERS FROM WITHIN

I feel the weight of breathless air surrounding me,

A fish upon the shore, gasping for peace.

In endless circles, searching for the sound,

Of answers that might let this turmoil cease.

My heart's a garden lost to thorns and haze,

Where lavender once bloomed, now shadows grow.

No more an open book on bright display,

I seek the solace that the hidden know.

Yet secrets buried deep within my chest,

Still pulse with life, refusing silent sleep.

A bond, a promise never laid to rest,

Its wound still bleeds a cut dark and deep.

I yearn to fade, to leave this world behind,

Forlorn, forgotten—peace in a quiet mind.

6. WHISKEY AND REGRETS

Guilt, love, lies, and other things that destroy you,

The dead cigarettes were once alive,

The weeds and the flowers were both beautiful,

But the weeds always won,

Aaahhh! That art of self-destruction.

Whiskey might have slit the throats,

What about love? Didn't it split the hearts?

You were all the seven wonders,

But I ain't no architect,

So you were nothing but a mess.

You had galaxies in your eyes,

But I ain't no astronaut.

You were the sunset and the sunrise,

All at once,

But I am that two-minute gap between them.

7. THE GREEK REMORSE

Mind was racing,

Heart was bruised!

Throat was slit,

And I was brutally murdered !!

I was stable, pale

But didn't bleed,

And was never buried.

I felt futile,

devastated and,

demented

I felt disoriented.

As Koalemos,

Perses,

Oizys,

Hail Eris.

Here I am,

Desolated in chaos,

Forlorn in soiree,

Extinct in extent.

It's all gloomy,

catastrophic,

effectuated,

And

All over!!!

8. THE WEIGHT OF MAYBE

She held her dead soul,

In her lifeless hands,

Two dead bodies, maybe?

She felt herself in mawsynram,

Waiting for the white snow to cover her,

And make her numb, maybe?

She felt herself in the badain jaran,

Waiting for the sand to cover her body,

And make her escape, maybe?

She wants to rest between his arms,

Just like her heart rests between her lungs,

Rest in peace, maybe?

What makes her throw everything around her,

What makes her scream louder,

Okay, that love, maybe?

Don't pick those tiny pieces of her heart,

Just let her be Dolores,

Just let it be!

Just let it be!

Just let it be, maybe!!!

9. BLEEDING POETRY

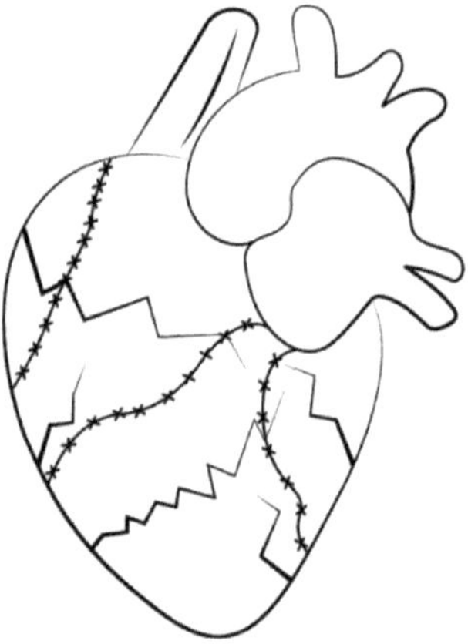

I find ways to hurt myself,

Be it by razors,

Or by your words, which cut deeper than a knife.

The blood on the razor satisfies me,

But those words of yours,

Oh my God! What an immense pleasure do they give,

As they cut my heart into pieces,

And that's when I bleed poetry.

I feel like a penguin,

Walking away from the sea, alone,

Towards my demise,

I am trying my best to meet it as soon as possible,

Moving forward to live in the harshest conditions,

Realizing I don't fit in this chaotic world.

Parting my ways from everyone I know,

And standing on the verge of hugging Azrael.

10. LOST

I sat there,

On the brink of losing everything,

Feeling as though I stood at the sprawling State Fair of Texas—

Surrounded by thousands, yet profoundly alone.

My presence felt as insignificant as the title of a forgotten film.

I was as lost as Alice in the depths of the Amazon,

Trying to navigate without a compass,

Running through the dense trees,

Only to arrive at nowhere.

The moon glowed like a solitary bulb in the sky,

Smoke lingered in the air like strands of candy floss.

Raindrops merged with my tears as they slipped from my face,

And there, I felt as lifeless as a doornail.

11. WILL YOU BE MINE?

I've had this question on my mind,

Troubling me for quite some time.

Can I tag someone in my heart?

Can I call him mine?

Hey love, are you listening? Will you be mine?

Hey love, are you watching? I'm dying.

Hey love, will you be there for dinner?

Hey love, will you let our hands entwine?

Can I call you mine?

Can we give it a fresh start?

Trust me, baby, I never wanted to part.

Can we be each other's Valentine?

Hey love, I love you—will you be mine?

Hey love, are you listening? Will you be mine?

Hey love, are you watching? I'm dying.

Hey love, will you be there for dinner?

Hey love, will you let our hands entwine?

Can I call you mine?

Can we stand by each other's side?

Because I want to be your bride.

Will you be my groom?

Because I want to share my room.

Hey love, I love you—will you be mine?

12. BEYOND THE REALM OF LOVE

Let's talk about everything except love.

Let's forget what's yours,

Let's forget what's mine,

Let's free our hands and let them entwine.

Let's talk about everything except love.

Let's not care about what happened,

Let's not worry about what's to come,

Let's sit here and watch the sky turn dark.

Let's talk about everything except love.

Let's ignore what's on your mind,

Let's ignore what's on mine,

Let's gaze at the stars that shine above.

Let's talk about everything except love.

Let's overlook your imperfections,

Just as you overlook mine,

Let's just savor the scent of wine.

Let's talk about everything except love.

Let's not discuss what you adore,

Let's not dwell on what I hate,

Let's ignore each other's every trait.

Let's talk about everything except love.

Let's not think about who's watching,

Let's not care who's judging,

Let's just do what makes us.

Let's talk about everything except love.

Let's ignore my big nose,

Let's overlook my imperfect brows,

Let's let our naked eyes get lost in the night.

Let's talk about everything except love.

Let the pouring rain drench our clothes,

Let my lips bridge the distance to yours,

Let's dance until our feet can't take any more.

Baby, let's talk about everything except love.

Let's forget what's yours,

Let's forget what's mine,

Let's free our hands and let them entwine.

13. ECHOES OF A SHATTERED HEART-I

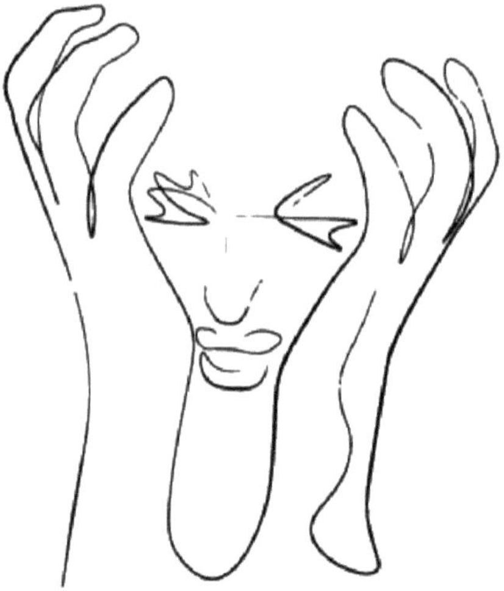

I hope this grief, a constant, should never fade,

As I embrace it, tenderly, with care.

It stirs the unspoken feelings in dark shades,

And fuels a hunger when others' joys are rare.

How many nights will these deep hauntings stay,

To caress me till indifference takes hold?

When will I cease to care, let shadows stray,

And silence the heart's beat, so harsh and cold?

I dread the flesh-bound pulse that drums so loud,

This suffocating world, a stifling chain.

My soul's afire, yet outside, I'm cowed,

A numbness wraps me, dulling all my pain.

If wounds must be felt, let them be mine alone,

In this cruel love that's turned my heart to stone.

14. ECHOES OF A SHATTERED HEART-II

I loved you as a dagger loves its mark,

Terror clings to cities torn by strife.

This love has scarred me, left me cold and dark,

Its jagged edges are carving out my life.

Arthur Miller's words I hold so dear,

"I'll cut my hand before I reach for you,"

The memories of us still draw near,

On calm nights when the ghosts of love pursue.

I remember too much of our past days,

This grief, this love with nowhere left to go,

It makes me vulnerable in endless ways,

As if my heart's been shattered in the throes.

Though I've let you go, you haunt me still,

In dreams where love's torment fits no one's will.

15. ECHOES OF A SHATTERED HEART-III

My love, you linger in my troubled mind,

A voice that haunts your calm and cozy nights.

Your clothes once drenched in the rain, you'll soon unwind,

And in my thoughts, you'll find no safe delights.

I'm not enraged, nor do I cast you blame,

It's simply pain that overwhelms my core.

My heart aches with plans I could not claim,

And tears, like unspent moments, I implore.

You could not grasp the depth of my devotion,

Nor see the spark that once ignited bright.

Now I howl in pain, a deep emotion,

A puzzle piece in someone else's light.

The love I had for you, a bitter scar,

It has left me weary, wondering who we are.

16. ECHOES OF A SHATTERED HEART-IV

I close my eyes to cry, a tender act,

When we kissed, both moments were pure and true.

Yet beautifying screams, a stark contract,

It might serve better than recalling moments with you.

To accept my place in others' lives, apart

Their short journeys leave me feeling small.

The thing that kept me alive now tears apart,

And silent death from waiting does befall.

You live beyond my pain, a path so grand,

While I felt destined for a lonely road.

Mahmoud Darwish's lines, like shifting sand,

Speak of my rebel heart, a heavy load.

I wish I could direct my heart's lament,

But peace eludes the broken heart's intent.

17. ECHOES OF A SHATTERED HEART-V

Love's sweetness, poets' dreams cannot convey,

It's like a rose with thorns that draws blood.

Its teeth can tear, its beauty fades away,

And leaves the heart in the depths of the gloomy flood.

I've given you a part too vital, dear,

A vital organ wrecked by your embrace.

My eyes are dark, foreboding skies near,

My heart's a blemished glass, a broken case.

I never thought you'd end what we had planned,

A universe where we could still exist.

This love, self-destruction's cruel reprimand,

Leaves me with nothing but a mournful twist.

In this fierce love, a fool's reward, I see,

A heart torn by a love that's left to bleed.

18. ECHOES OF A SHATTERED HEART-VI

I'm weary now of suffering day and night,

Each word I speak, each pain I choose to bear.

Memories of us rise, a stark twilight,

With solitude, my silent cross to wear.

Your life's unburdened by this endless woe,

You walked a path that stretched so far and wide.

While I, the sole one bound to sorrow's flow,

Bear all the weight of love I cannot hide.

Peace be upon my broken heart and soul,

This love, a rose with thorns and teeth so keen.

In every pause, I strive to take control,

Yet I remain in darkness, lost, unseen.

The love I knew, a self-destructive flame,

It is now my sorrow and my heart's true claim.

19. THE FADING COLORS OF MY STORY

She met me in the days of my dilapidation,

She painted the walls with colors of hope,

Her hair gradually became the strings to my fingers,

And her smile, my reason to live.

We stood firm and wove a tapestry,

In her eyes, I found the reflection of every dream I had,

Her laughter was the cure for all my silent nights,

And her voice was a soft echo in my barren land.

In the calmest of nights, when the world was asleep,

The rhythm of her heart made me weep,

Her breaths were a gentle reminder,

To make me stare at the winder.

But the stare made a thief creep into our world,

Her hair, once a string to my finger, fell away,

Her laughter, once a cure for my silent nights, grew faint,

Her voice, once a soft echo to my barren land, started to fade.

The walls once painted with hope ghost me now,

Her love, still strong, yet a distant memory somehow,

She slipped into a place where I couldn't follow,

And she left me in utmost dilapidation.

I must say she was strained to do so,

But the void of her absence can't be filled,

Our tapestry can't be woven again,

The dreams we shared now drift away.

I linger in the echoes of what used to be,

Haunted by the love that slipped from me,

A love that only lives in memory,

Forever etched in the shadows of my heart.

I was unable to reveal her veil,

I was unable to make our ship sail,

Dreams of forever now had swiftly denied,

And it was a silent death.

20. THE THOUGHTS WITHIN

In the hours of profound solitude,

I dream of a canvas, pristine and untouched.

It would bear the brushstrokes of muted tones—

Ash, slate, anchor, smoke, porpoise, and charcoal—

A harmonious flow to mend the fractured soul.

You did not intend cruelty, I concede,

Yet the bruxism and shivers reveal a harsher truth.

"My grief accompanies you," it murmurs,

And I am left to exist merely,

Suspended in the interstice of hope and resignation.

In this cold expanse, I contemplate rebirth,

A fresh beginning on a blank, unmarred canvas.

Where colors blend in a soothing rhythm,

Transforming the disarray of pain into something coherent.

As I navigate this labyrinth of existence,

I grapple with the chilling knowledge

That to love and lose is to be profoundly changed.

In the quiet aftermath, all I can do is exist—

An echo of a life once vibrant, now subdued.

21. SILENCE

In silence, where words falter,

I grapple with feelings too complex to name.

Does every bruised heart once know kindness?

Are all heart birds trapped in ribbed cages,
yearning for liberation?

Sometimes, I wonder if a knife's wound might sting less

Than the piercing weight of your words,

For I am trapped in a familiar desolation,

A place where I feel Alice Oseman's words ring true—

"Sometimes I think if nobody spoke to me, I'd never speak again."

Why do I succumb to this relentless sorrow?

An answer eludes me, slipping through the cracks

During sleepless nights spent in grief's embrace,

Nurturing it with a paradoxical pleasure.

It is disquieting to see others falter

When I voice my unease, a plea they cannot fathom.

My fears were once the heights and depths;

Now, I am haunted by the dread of losing someone and in turn, losing myself.

Love fades for reasons it once flourished,

The stubbornness of affection becomes a weighty compromise.

Surroundings grow chill, hands shiver,

An existential cold settling deep within.

22. HIS MAGIC

The weather in my heart was solitary and lonely,

Until he emerged as the beacon of joy.

His eyes light up with an unmatched brilliance,

A gleam that eclipses the darkness within.

I had sealed off my inner self,

A sanctuary shut even to my longing.

Yet, he found his way to that hidden core,

Navigating the labyrinth of my soul with ease.

Daily, I dream of a future entwined with him,

His presence is a balm to my fractured spirit.

He has reconciled me with my essence,

Resting within my despondent heart.

No longer do I yearn to escape what I cherish;

He has become an integral part of my being.

In contemplating and conversing with him,

I sense myself fading, losing my identity.

New yet familiar, we are as though never estranged,

His mere words penetrate to my very core.

He approaches, and I find myself poised to transform him into poetry,

The epitome of all I could ever wish for.

23. SERENADE OF THE SOUL

I envision him adorned in light,

Wrapped in a cloak of acceptance,

Longing for every facet of his being,

Drenched in empathy and endless tenderness.

His words resonate like soothing waves

Crashing gently against rocks on a serene summer eve.

His eyes, profound as the ocean's depths,

And that smile—oh, it steals my breath away.

His gaze chills me as if my soul were a wanderer's feet

On a snowy evening, frozen in time.

He has permeated my being, tending to its scars

Without reopening the wounds.

Amidst the clamor of the world,

I seek solace in his embrace,

A sanctuary found in his presence,

Where the cacophony of life fades into peaceful quiet.

24. THE DESOLATION WITHIN

A longing to decipher the stories in each gaze,

An endless quest to capture silent truths.

The more I write, the deeper my craving,

Each line is a step closer to understanding.

He may loathe the smile unseen through my eyes,

But does he value the reflection within mine?

I wish to honor the grief that keeps me alive,

To acknowledge those crushed by neglect.

Support feels distant; emotions leave me weary,

How does one move on from a phantom love?

Each confession has laid me bare,

Seeing others where I once ached.

Ignoring the storm of my feelings seems futile,

A storm that raged within, now silent.

I hope he someday grasps the depth of my gaze,

And regrets not seeing the soul that once yearned.

25. THOUGHTS BEFORE A STORM

A peculiar silence has knocked within me,

Or perhaps, it's a storm rising in the depths.

Does the stillness before a storm render waves powerless?

The joy of someone's arrival or the sorrow of their departure,

Why do those moments always seem greater?

Is living on memories so very difficult?

Perhaps yes, or maybe nothing is simpler.

The trembling hands that write reveal a different story.

I knew him, examined him, understood him,

Yet the fear of losing him outweighs the joy of having him.

An odd pain rises within my chest,

Are incomplete stories truly better?

They may be, but I need my completeness,

Good or bad, I require my entirety.

If it's bad, my faith lies in making it better,

This is the truth; this is the second belief I hold.

My tongue may be silenced,

But my eyes speak all that my tongue cannot.

My condition may be evident to them,

Yet they are naive, blind, and ignorant.

What can they understand of the storm within?

A person is a grave unto themselves; only they know their condition.

Why does everything remind me of them?

Is it the silence or the storm that makes me cry or keeps me alive?

This storm has shaken my mental focus,

I am terrified—of myself, of him, of this yearning.

And of this world, where some people are huge barriers between us,

I have placed my hope in meeting him only with my Lord.

The storm cannot sink my vessel,

And no one but my Lord can bring me to him.

People's words have distanced me from myself,

I am so very tired now; my courage has read its past,

And I am slowly fading away.

26. THE SILENT LAMENT-1

In labyrinths of melancholy's woe,

My spirit falters, courage all but spent,

With pathos deep and heart laid bare, I know

A storm brews where solace is absent.

The sorrow swells within my tortured mind,

As anger's tide grows fiercer day by day,

In suffocating gloom, I am confined,

And through this dark, my essence finds its way.

I yearned to be a vault where secrets sleep,

A refuge for confessions, pure and deep,

Yet none were hidden, and the silence weeps,

For promises once held are now too steep.

Thus, in despair's embrace, I wish to fade,

My soul's lament a shadow's masquerade.

27. THE SILENT LAMENT-2

Within the confines of a sorrowful heart,

A wound persists where once a promise lay,

To bury what was vital from the start,

Now, it festers in the ruins of dismay.

A bond once treasured is now an open scar,

Unkept and buried while it should have breathed,

Its essence haunts like a forsaken star,

A ghostly tether, with my spirit sheathed.

I am the crypt of hopes that failed to last,

A shelter for confessions gone awry,

With every thought, I relive the past,

And in this solitude, I yearn to die.

For in forlornness, my soul finds its flight,

In desolation, seeking endless night.

28. THE SAND AND WATER

Upon the water, words dissolve in waves,

In sand, each grain inscribes its tale.

From word to word, their echoes are unbound,

And memories from memories grow pale.

What grievous wrong that people cease to be,

And friends dissolve as shadows in the dusk.

We, too, are lost, our essence swept to sea,

And in this haze, your memory starts to musk.

For as I lost my mental strength and grace,

Your visage surfaced through the fog of time.

I see the cost of trying to erase,

The sacrifice of moments so sublime.

In vain, I sought to leave the past behind,

Yet written deep, your memory's intertwined.

29. WAIT

Is each waiting span forever too long?

Does every pause stretch into an endless night?

The truth of waiting lies where hearts belong,

In those who bear the weight of longing's fight.

A chest of words I held but could not write,

For feelings tangled in unspoken seams.

Though I could not unveil them to the light,

Their echoes lived within my hidden dreams.

You were my world, envisioned day by day,

Yet, now I face the journey to forget.

A love so deep, it haunts me in its sway,

A struggle to let go, to not regret.

In darkest hours, desires intertwine,

Where night conceals the truth from dawn's harsh glare.

The daylight casts my dreams in stark design,

And shows the wreckage of a love laid bare.

Yes, every wait is long and fraught with pain,

But mine, I fear, eclipses all the rest.

30. THE CONFINEMENT

This confinement grows tighter with each day,

The moment of judgment feels imminent,

Caught in a strange struggle of my own making,

Alive, yet it seems I am not truly living.

Lost in a gathering of hollow revelry,

I would join them, but the path is strewn with obstacles,

To speak out may bring scorn upon myself,

To ask may risk a fate worse than death.

My condition is complex and tangled,

My hair falls in disarray,

My head hangs low in weariness,

My lips are parched, untouched by ease.

This confinement tightens evermore,

And the hour of decision draws near,

Its arrival now felt in every breath,

A burden that intensifies with each fleeting moment.

31. THE TRIALS AND TRIBULATIONS

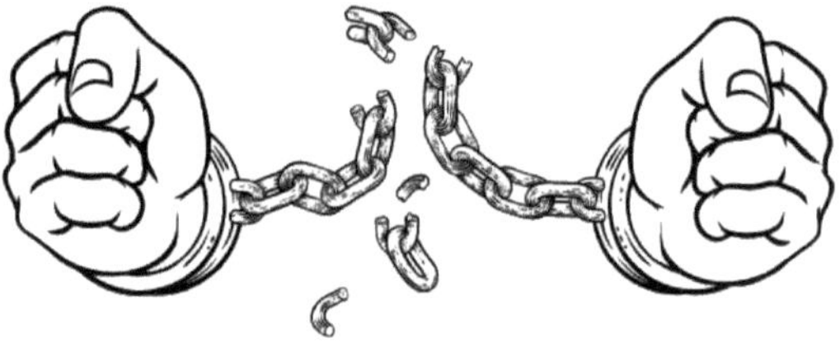

My endurance had overflowed,

And I had forgotten that not every battle must be fought.

Even if fought, not every struggle assures victory.

That day, my war was against myself,

A fierce contest following a profound defeat.

I had placed every plea within my prayers,

Perhaps it was an undue burden upon him,

My fate entwined with battles

That seemed beyond the realm of victory.

I could not fully embrace my defeat,

My patience was stretched and tested,

Until it shattered, and my endurance waned

I was overwhelmed by the weight of trials.

32. THE SILENCE BEFORE THE STORM

An uncanny quiet has settled inside me,

Or perhaps a storm brews in the stillness.

The prelude to a storm renders waves helpless,

As if they, too, are ensnared by impending fury.

How do moments before joy or grief measure up?

Are memories a weighty burden to carry?

Maybe so, or perhaps they are less arduous than they seem.

My trembling hands narrate an untold story.

I discovered him, studied him,

Yet the dread of losing him surpassed

The fleeting joy of having him.

An unusual ache pervades my chest.

Do unfinished stories hold a certain charm?

I think they might, but I seek my wholeness.

Good or ill, I want the entirety,

A belief that prayer can transform the bad into good.

My silence might seem deafening,

Yet my eyes betray what my words cannot express.

My condition might reveal all to those who care,

But they are blind to the storm within me.

Human limitations blind us to internal tempests,

Only the heart truly knows its depth.

My longing for reunion surpasses worldly barriers,

Only my Creator can bridge this chasm.

This storm won't claim my vessel,

And none but my Lord can bring us together.

Words and judgments have alienated me from myself,

I am profoundly tired, and my spirit is near its end.

33. UNSPOKEN NUANCES

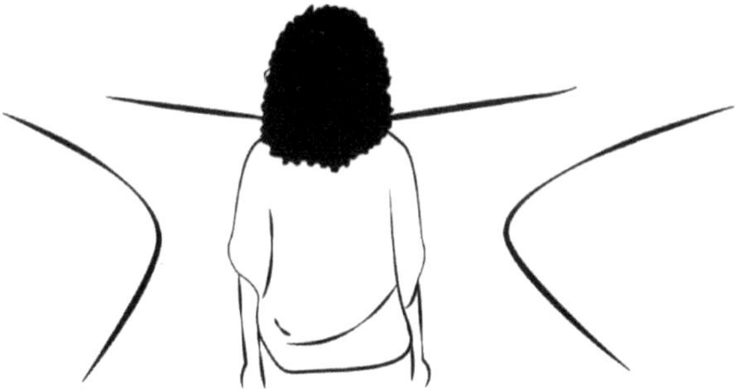

Some tales, some fragments, seem to hold their grace,

Pages left unturned can still enchant the mind.

To recall or to forget is a separate case,

Yet some things dwell most beautifully confined.

I chose not to know some hearts too near,

For knowing them wholly might just leave a scar.

To be unaware and to keep things clear,

Is different from making a journey too far.

In words uttered or unuttered, I reside,

In my conscience and my resolve, they linger.

The nuances and the subtleties, untried,

When did I truly ponder, the value of these?

When did I discern their weight and worth,

The difference in their measure and their mirth?

34. A TRANQUIL COLLAPSE

In the maze of our profound despair,

Where shadows twist in sorrow's snare,

We encounter marks that time has sown,

The silent hurts that remain unknown.

To love completely, to lose the fight,

And vanish from the edge of sight;

No cries are heard, no tears are shed—

A gentle fall, a quiet thread.

Our hearts quake within their depth,

Revealing every flaw and breath,

Yet, in our fury and trembling state,

Lies the truth of love's dying fate.

In affection, vulnerability is exposed,

Each embrace, a truth that's enclosed,

Preference for another's plea,

Becomes a sign of a soul's decree.

Today, fatigue unveiled a truth so clear,

That weariness goes beyond mere fear,

For in sorrow's grasp, we find the strain,

That drains the spirit in joy and pain.

35. FRAGMENTS OF LOVE

In love, we forsake our judgments, preferring the beloved above all else.

To raise a voice in anger or harbor discontent is merely a testament to our strength—or lack thereof.

In the quiet corners of our hearts, fragility becomes evident,

A recognition of how deeply love can enfeeble and bind us.

We forget the cries of our struggles as we dissolve in devotion.

Even when we are shattered and scattered,

Our thoughts remain tethered to the beloved.

In love's all-encompassing hold,

We lose ourselves, letting it consume our very essence.

36. THE ODD HOUR

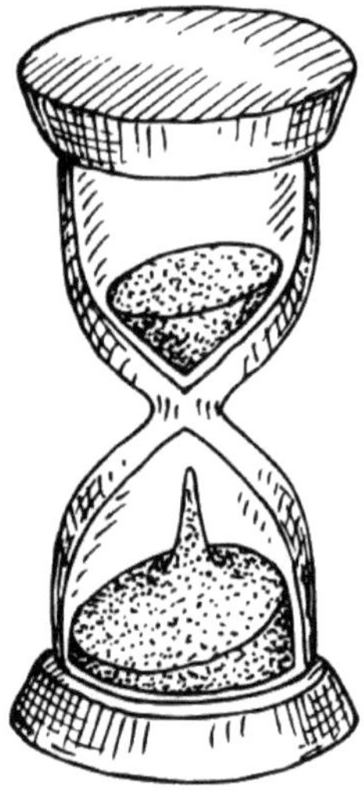

In the depth of night's embrace,

Where shadows weave their silent threads,

I search for answers long obscured,

lost in the vastness of this darkened hour.

My conscience, restless, resists the pull,

Yet in the veil of darkness, what is wrong seems easy to grasp.

The true cost of love is clear—the surrender of self-respect.

Some cling fiercely to their honor,

While others surrender and are trampled upon.

In this obscurity, we lose ourselves

In the echo of our unspoken fears.

We meet ourselves in the quiet,

Discussing with our reflections,

A battle unfolds between heart and mind,

No visible conflict, only silent decisions.

37. THE TRUTHS UNSPOKEN

If only we had met like we were meant to,

If only you had come as you were expected.

If only I had found you as one finds a cherished goal,

If only you had desired me as one loves earnestly.

Rivers do dry up in their time,

Leaves do fall as seasons shift,

People do break, and promises do die,

In this world where nothing remains the same.

Daily, I embark on this journey alone,

Living life as best as I can.

The joy of finding you is one thing,

But the fear of losing you is a different torment.

My heartbeat quickened,

And my breaths seemed to freeze.

It felt as though that cold night,

With its fierce winds and gentle rain,

Had shared some unspoken truth with me.

A question lingered,

Wrapping around my heart and mind:

Would you return, or would you not?

In solitude, I searched for an answer,

Haunted by that cold night, the fierce winds, and the gentle rain,

And a heart heavy with despair.

38. A DREAM UNFULFILLED

This heart of stone is slowly being shattered,

Or perhaps it has already been entirely broken.

Life is entangled in your dark tresses,

I am weary from gathering the fragments of your memory.

Now I yearn for stillness,

To leave behind these memories and vanish far away,

To a place where even your echoes cannot reach.

Caught in a relentless struggle,

My life feels estranged,

With only your memories as my companion,

While you remain distant and unfaithful.

I dreamt of building a home with you,

Of setting the birds free, yet keeping you bound.

I longed for your presence to be mine forever,

To hold you close in my heart,

And to sever ties with the world,

To confine you within the depths of my being.

I envisioned a shared life together,

But now, all that remains is the weight of shattered hopes,

And the unfulfilled dream of a home that was never ours.

39. THE TORN PAGES

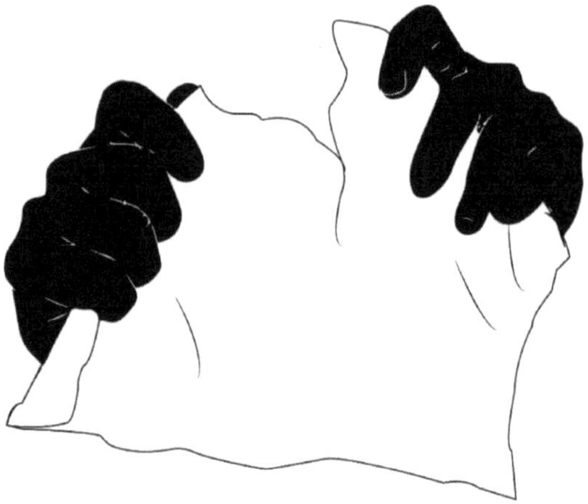

The revelation that the one you once loved is a stranger,

Feels like a cold wind on a scorched land.

Flowers and flames, help in the process of forgetting,

Each with its narrative, each with its weight.

The fire within us needs a keeper,

An actuator to temper its fierce blaze.

I've amassed bandages over time,

Not realizing that love's wounds don't bleed—they break.

The pain is a deep fissure, beyond sight and understanding.

My grief, my pain, and my sorrow are a tapestry,

Wrapping me until it begins to suffocate.

I escaped into my creation,

Hiding within the depths of my mind.

Protecting myself from myself—how naive.

Exhausted despite rest,

Trust issues seep into my core,

A tendency to retreat into silence.

As Hanif Abdurraqib put it,

"I can't live as I once did,"

I am no longer soft, warm, or kind.

I have become hardened, stronger, darker—beyond view.

I reside in your thoughts, a wound that won't heal,

A piece you can't abandon,

In pain, I find my peculiar peace,

For it is only through suffering that I feel truly alive.

40. LAVENDER

Ah, the lavender—its soothing scent they claim,

Yet what if its promise fails to calm my unrest?

What if I seek tranquility not in blooms,

But in a garden sown within your thoughts?

Imagine a grove dense enough to trap,

A labyrinth of green thriving in the recesses of your mind.

Can you unravel my intricate designs?

What if I nurture the flowers in my deepest sorrow,

Allowing them to blossom where sadness dwells?

What if the autumn's lesson teaches me to release you,

And I yearn for a Juliet rose,

Imagining you as its thorny embrace?

What if the branches, with their patient strength,

Guide me in the art of waiting?

What if my questions unravel the delicate knots

Tied tightly in your chest, leaving them loosened forever?

What if I show you how to bleed poetry,

Transforming pain into beauty?

What if I make your heart race and hands tremble,

Teaching you to find grace within anxiety?

What if, in letting you know,

I create a masterpiece from the disquiet of my mind,

A garden of elegance flourishing amidst the turmoil?

41. FOREVER

Have you pondered the time it takes to dismantle,

To obliterate something or someone?

What about the concept of forever?

What comes to mind when you hear the word "FOREVER"?

How long does forever span?

Is the notion of eradication tied to its endlessness?

Do I seem like a Pantomath to you?

Perhaps, but consider: does destruction require more than a fleeting moment?

Is forever a land of blissful endings,

Or merely a fleeting instance in the grand scheme?

How do you define love?

To me, it seems an illusion,

Maybe a parallel universe's fiction,

While what remains is obsession,

A force laden with a weight all its own.

Is it heavier than the rest of our emotions?

Do we each craft our own philosophies of love and desire,

With stories of ifs and buts,

Tales of love, betrayal, and relentless obsession?

Tell me, how does betrayal feel?

And what of being the betrayer?

Does guilt weigh heavily on every traitor's heart?

Is seeking attention a transgression in itself?

For me, an obsessor may cross any boundary

In the name of their fervent longing,

For in obsession, limits dissolve,

And the heart's relentless chase knows no bounds.

42. DESIRES AND DENIAL

In the stillness of my soul, a quiet murmur grows,

No one seems to grasp it, nor do I wish them to—

Perhaps it's a longing, a gentle, hidden pain,

Where the world's understanding feels like distant rain.

Do you find comfort in the pity of your own plight,

Believing that none truly see or know your inner fight?

Yet, do you grasp yourself, in truth, in clear sight,

Or is it all a child's play, with essence lost at night?

Let's leave behind these petty whims, these childish games,

And question what lies ahead beyond these dim flames.

You never wished for me, nor did I long for you;

Caught in this binding, our paths are nothing new.

Desire and denial, mere fragments of our plight,

But to seek divine grace might ignite a light.

If I release these trivial woes, what remains for us both?

In this devotion's madness, have we taken an oath?

To mourn in silence, to wander in your memory's hold,

With hearts wounded deeply, with stories left untold.

Some may strike their heads in frustration, others cut their hands,

Yet, in these acts of folly, have you ever made plans?

To abandon the lost in their search for meaning and grace,

Is to leave them adrift, with no sanctuary or place.

I bid farewell to these acts of foolish despair,

Yet, don't leave me alone in this emptiness laid bare.

43. REST IN PEACE

I wish I could sever this throat, let it spill

The torrent of emotions, raw and untamed.

To set them free from this vessel,

To let them drift away, to breathe and then dissolve.

These feelings, burdensome and relentless,

Bind me with their invisible chains.

If only I could cut this conduit,

And watch the pain flow out, unshackled.

To release these shadows from their prison,

To cleanse them in the open air,

To watch them vanish,

Not as an end, but as a release.

I dream of a quiet emptiness,

Where the weight of sorrow is gone,

Where emotions no longer haunt,

Where silence is not filled with echoes of anguish.

In this space, unburdened and light,

I seek a tranquil departure.

To sever, to release,

To let these feelings find their final rest.

44. THE UNREAD LETTER

I wish I could turn back the pages,

To a place where the fear of losing you never existed,

Where hope was a constant, an unshakable beacon,

And the weight of loss was a distant thought.

Here, there's nothing left to lose—

The night's murmurs, the morning's whispers,

The entanglements of the day, the fading twilight,

Each moment feels like a test, a question without an answer.

The dawn offers a fleeting hope,

Yet the dusk shakes me with harsh reality.

The letter you never read

Held the essence of my life's despair,

A tale of separation, untold and unwritten,

A sorrow too deep for words, too profound for ink.

Now, only one longing remains—

A story of a heart in despair,

A plea unheard, a cry to be known.

Shall I shout this tale out to the world,

The tale of a life I am bound to endure?

The sorrows, the restlessness,

The fading promises, the madness—

Which song shall I sing for you?

Which letter shall I write?

In the end, let my suffering be yours,

My nights of blood be reflected in yours,

My mornings of pain, in your dawn.

Let my name alone be spoken,

As your life turns into a reflection of my yearning.

45. THE UNRAVELED VIEL

Let lives drift away, their essence unraveling,

If only one would yield, I'd secure the other—

Offering you the veil of my name,

Does it matter if it stays white or turns red?

The prayer beads have shattered,

The pearls have fallen,

The village has been plundered,

The sanctuary burned to the ground.

The ship has sunk,

The riders have perished,

The river has dried up,

The trees have fallen.

The seeds we once sowed

Have withered away,

The soil has scattered,

And our emotions have crumbled.

What remains of beauty in the remnants,

Hidden truths lie beneath your gaze.

If only I could let you see the lives that have slipped away,

If only I could offer you the veil of my name.

Does it matter if it stays white or turns red?

46. THE BELATED RETURN

Hasten your return, for solitude is unbearable,

I find myself envying every heart that holds you close,

And who, now, is the recipient of your affection?

This isolation relentlessly gnaws at my resolve,

And darkness derides me with its mocking gaze.

Though I strive to remain patient, my heart protests,

Battered and subdued, I am apprehensive at your absence.

Never have I shed such torrents of sorrow,

Bearing numerous wounds and heavy burdens of blame.

The scars upon my soul are many,

And the accusations are not few,

In this vast expanse, acquaintances are scant.

So return promptly, for this seclusion is untenable,

And my spirit can no longer withstand the weight of solitude.

47. THE UNANSWERED QUESTIONS

Do you ever find hope slipping away,

As you return to the harsh light of reality,

Leaving behind the world you've spun in your mind,

The fantasies where every trial was a triumph?

Do you face situations far graver than imagined,

Where the courage you envisioned remains elusive?

Is the person you envisioned standing steadfast

Or do they vanish with reasons that seem valid, yet hollow?

Will they endure the trials beside you,

Or leave you alone to grapple with unanticipated burdens?

Will they uphold the promises you dreamed of,

Or transform into another enigma, shrouded in secrecy?

Will they defend you as you had hoped,

Or will their support wane under pressure,

Contrary to the image you had crafted in your heart?

Will their words ring true, or will they prove to be mere echoes of deceit?

Will their affection remain as you had envisioned,

Or will it fade with the mounting challenges?

You search for answers to these profound questions,

Yet find yourself wishing for escape before confronting the reality of it all.

48. TALE OF A FRAGMENTED PAST

As time unraveled, what remained was bare,

A canvas stripped of colors, threads of despair,

You took away more than words could convey,

My craft, my fight, my voice, now frayed.

In the twilight of memories, I was left to muse,

On fragments of a life, scattered and bruised,

You claimed my pen, my passion's fire,

Left me with echoes of a once fierce desire.

What I received in return were shadows alone,

Fleeting whispers, and echoes of a past overgrown,

Images of moments that once held meaning,
Now haunt my nights, in restless, silent dreaming.

I find myself weary, drained of all zeal,

Every page I turned, a void left to reveal,

Each story I wove, every thought that was shared,

Was crafted in the fabric of a heart that cared.

The weight of my past, with its pain and its grace,

Now sits upon me, an unending embrace,

For I burdened my tale with love and with sorrow,

And now bear the strain of what remains tomorrow.

The deeds done were harsh, a toll too steep,

I laid waste to a dream that I could not keep,

In the ruins of this story, I now dwell,

A silent witness to the echoes that swell.

So here I stand, at the edge of this fray,

Worn and weary, with no more to say,

My tale, once vibrant, now softly fades,

In the quiet of memories, where the past cascades.

49. INNER CONFLICT

In the depths where shadows weave their shroud,

I dwell amidst a tempest fierce and proud,

Where delicate daisies and diamonds alike,

Fall victim to my restless, roving strike.

Each heartbeat is a tremor of undone grace,

Unveiling wounds in the quietest space,

Where silence and sorrow share their place,

And words are fraught with an empty embrace.

The echoes of laughter, or the pangs of despair,

Mingle in a void, an uncharted lair,

I'm adrift in a sea of tumultuous mien,

Wrestling with a truth that remains unseen.

What do these souls truly yearn to possess?

Is it the dark allure of loneliness' caress?

Or perhaps the fleeting joy that laughter bestows,

In the paradox of existence, where uncertainty grows?

Hearts fractured and fraught with endless strain,

Stand as monuments to relentless pain,

Enduring what others falter to bear,

Without remorse, they have burdens to share.

Confined within a world of claustrophobic lore,

They see themselves as rare, precious, and more,

Gems of discord, caught in a ceaseless fray,

Their existence is a battlefield where shadows play.

Escaping into realms of darkened dreams,

They find solace in the abyssal seam,

Where reality's light fails to pierce the veil,

And each descent into darkness unveils.

Their garden of lavender, meant to soothe,

Reveals that not all remedies are smooth,

For wounds remain despite their fragrant hue,

As they wander the maze of what is and what they know.

In this woven fabric of sorrow and hope,

They seek a dawn where true serenity might elope,

Yet, in every shadowed corner of their plight,

They confront their ghosts in the ceaseless night.

Each step dances on the fractured ground,

Where threads of anguish and anticipation are found,

In the tapestry of existence, dark and fraught,

They await a dawn that remains elusive, caught.

50. THE CLOSURE

As the last page turns, the ink dries still,

The echoes of our verses find their tranquil fill,

In the silence that follows, the words softly lay,

A testament to the journey of this poetic array.

In this bound volume, where dreams have soared,

We've danced with shadows and light explored,

Each page a canvas, each word a guide,

Leading through emotions, deep and wide.

In the rhythm of stanzas, in the pulse of rhyme,

We've found fragments of solace, moments sublime,

Each verse a mirror, each line a thread,

Woven into the fabric of dreams we've read.

The words have danced in the spaces between,

In the quiet moments where dreams are seen,

From the dawn of inspiration to twilight's grace,

We've navigated the realms of the soul's vast space.

Though the book now closes, the echoes remain,

In the chambers of hearts where the verses sustain,

For in every poem, a piece of us stays—

A testament to the journey through these poetic days.

Printed by Libri Plureos GmbH in Hamburg,
Germany

9 789363 3055